KLONDIKE HO!

A CARTOON HISTORY

WRITTEN AND ILLUSTRATED BY
CURTIS VOS

Lost Moose Publishing • Whitehorse, Yukon • 1994

Published by Lost Moose Publishing, Whitehorse, Yukon, Canada

Canadian Cataloguing in Publication Data

Vos, Curtis, 1968-
    Klondike ho!

    Includes bibliographical references.
    ISBN 0-9694612-4-0

    1. Klondike River Valley (Yukon)—Gold discoveries—Comic
books, strips, etc. 2. Comic books, strips, etc, Canadian
(English) * I. Title.

FC4022.3.V67 1994   971.9'02'0207   C94-910427-2
F1095.K5V67 1994

Printed and bound in Canada

For information on this and other books from Lost Moose Publishing see back of book.

CONTENTS

CHAPTER 1

THE BIG DISCOVERY   1

CHAPTER 2

THE RACE IS ON   13

CHAPTER 3

THE CHILKOOT PASS   27

CHAPTER 4

BOOMTOWN   41

CHAPTER 5

ONE GOLDEN YEAR   55

THE BIG DISCOVERY

I panned and I panned in the shiny sand, and I sniped on the river shore;
But I know, I know, that it's down below that the golden treasures are;
So I'll wait and I'll wait till the floods abate and I'll sink a shaft once more,
And I'd like to bet that I'll go home yet with a brass band playing before

"Clancy of the mounted police"
Robert Service

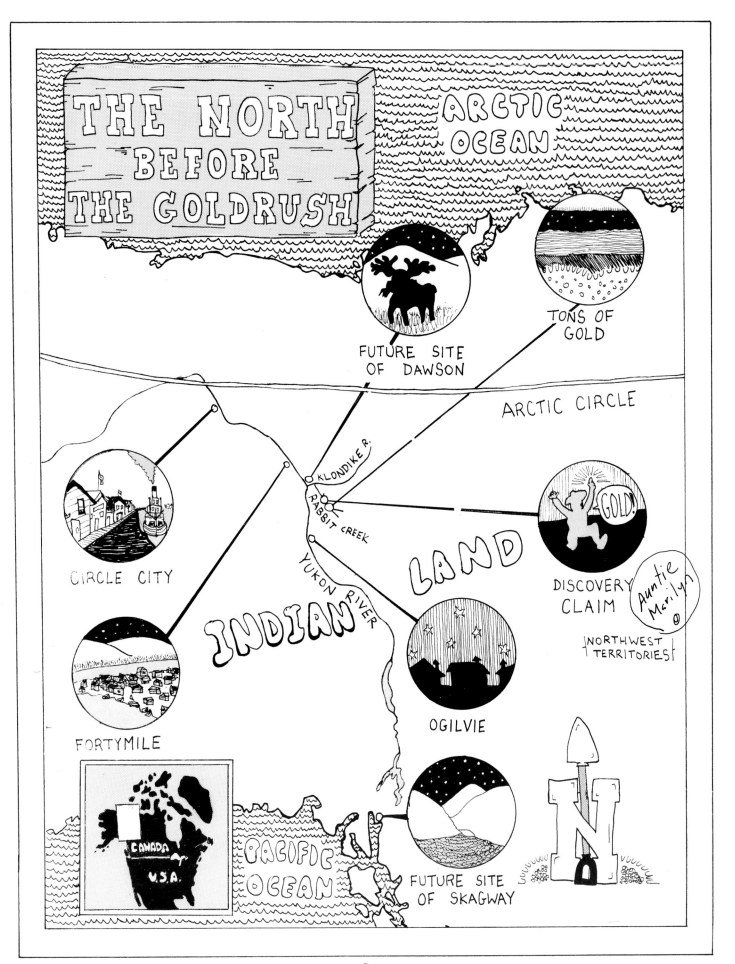

IN THE BEGINNING...

FOR THOUSANDS OF YEARS THE VAST NORTHLANDS WERE THE SOLE DOMAIN OF MIGRATING MAMMALS & NATIVE INDIANS, BUT IN THE COURSE OF A YEAR THIS LAND WOULD BE TEEMING WITH OVER 100,000 WHITE PEOPLE MAD WITH THAT MOST PECULIAR OF ILLNESSES: **GOLD FEVER**

IN THE LATER HALF OF THE 1800s, PROSPECTORS BEGAN TO TRICKLE INTO THE WILD NORTH, SOME OF THEM VETERANS OF THE CALIFORNIA & CARIBOU COUNTRY GOLD RUSHES

RUMBLE

LIVING "NORTH OF 60°" WAS NO PICNIC, WHAT WITH PANNING FOR GOLD IN FRIGID CREEKS...

& WORKING UNDERGROUND IN SMOKEY MINES

OUCH!

NOT THAT CABIN LIFE WAS MUCH BETTER...

OUCH!

3

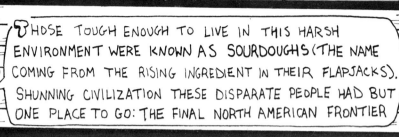

NORTHERN MINING TOWNS

Those tough enough to live in this harsh environment were known as sourdoughs (the name coming from the rising ingredient in their flapjacks). Shunning civilization these disparate people had but one place to go: the final North American frontier

By 1896, 3 major log cabin towns lined the 2,000 mile Yukon River

The sourdoughs were a breed apart, rugged & often eccentric

The mining towns were glutted with thieving sled dogs,

But sled dogs were not the only pets preferred by some prospectors

There were no laws save those passed by "miners' meetings"

SORRY, MINERS ONLY

For to survive in this desolate corner of the world, only 1 rule need apply:

THE GOLDEN RULE, OF COURSE!

DRINKS ON ME

Another characteristic the prospectors shared was an insurmountable desire to strike the motherlode of gold... THE ELDORADO!

GEORGE CARMACK   "SKOOKUM" JIM

It would be these two unlikely characters who would do just that...

THE FATEFUL MEETING

GEORGE CARMACK HAD ARRIVED IN THE YUKON IN 1885 & HAD MARRIED AN INDIAN CHIEF'S DAUGHTER, KATE. WITH HIS BROTHERS-IN-LAW, "SKOOKUM" JIM & "TAGISH" CHARLIE HE HAD BEEN A PACKER & A FISHERMAN. HOWEVER, UNLIKE MOST IN THE LAND, HE CARED LITTLE FOR PROSPECTING...

THE THREESOME WAS SMOKING SALMON AT THE JUNCTION OF THE KLONDIKE & YUKON RIVERS...

WHEN A SMALL BOAT CARRYING VETERAN PROSPECTOR ROBERT HENDERSON DRIFTED INTO VIEW

Yo GEORGE

HOWDY BOB, WHAT BRINGS YOU THIS WAY?

FOUND A GOOD PROSPECT IN A SMALL CREEK UP RIVER

HMMMM... ANYTHING WORTH STAKING?

SURE, FOR YOU GEORGE... BUT LEAVE THOSE DAMN INDIANS HERE

!

WHAT MATTER DAT WHITE MAN? HIM KILL INDIAN MOOSE, CATCH GOLD IN INDIAN COUNTRY, NO LIKE INDIAN STAKE CLAIM?! WHAT FOR, NO GOOD!

NEVERMIND JIM, THIS IS A BIG COUNTRY. WE'LL GO FIND A CREEK OF OUR OWN...

WITH THAT SAID, OFF THEY WENT...

DISCOVERY DAY

FROM THE MOUTH OF THE KLONDIKE RIVER THE TRIO TRUDGED TOWARDS THE AREA OF HENDERSON'S CLAIM, MILDLY CURIOUS. TAKING AN ALTERNATIVE ROUTE BY WAY OF RABBIT CREEK, THEY OCCASIONALLY PANNED THE WATERS, FINDING MINUTE GOLD FRAGMENTS...

AFTER SEVERAL DAYS THEY CAME UPON HENDERSON'S STRIKE...

LET'S GO SEE WHAT HE'S GOT

BUT THE PROSPECTS FAILED TO EXCITE GEORGE...

THANKS BOB, BUT WE'RE HEADING BACK NOW

LET ME KNOW IF YOU FIND ANYTHING

THE TRIO RETRACED THEIR STEPS, UNAWARE THAT THEY WERE WALKING ON THE RICHEST CONCENTRATION OF GOLD IN THE WORLD; HERE THEY MADE CAMP...

HERE THE STORY GETS BLURRED, FOR BOTH GEORGE & JIM CLAIM TO HAVE FOUND THE FIRST NUGGET

BUT IT MATTERS LITTLE WHO FOUND IT, THE GOLD WAS THERE "THICK AS CHEESE"!

THE NEXT DAY GEORGE WENT TO REGISTER THE CLAIM, TELLING EVERYONE HE MET ABOUT THE STRIKE...

BUT HE DID NOT SEND WORD TO ROBERT HENDERSON...

HENDERSON, HIS BIGOTRY COSTING HIM DEARLY, WOULD NOT HEAR ABOUT THE STRIKE FOR MONTHS...

BY THEN THE BEST LAND WAS ALREADY CLAIMED!

LYING GEORGE

SINCE ONLY WHITES COULD REGISTER CLAIMS, OFF WENT GEORGE CARMACK TO THE TOWN OF FORTYMILE. HERE IN TOWN HE WAS KNOWN AS "LYING GEORGE" BECAUSE OF HIS TALL TALES, BUT THIS WAS ABOUT TO CHANGE...

BEFORE REGISTERING HIS CLAIM, GEORGE WENT TO HAVE A DRINK

LOOK, HERE COMES OL' LYIN' GEORGE

HEY GEORGE, FIND ANY GOLD LATELY?

SNICKER

ACTUALLY GUYS, GUESS WHAT? I JUST MADE A HUGE STRIKE UP RIVER.

YEAH, SURE... PROVE IT

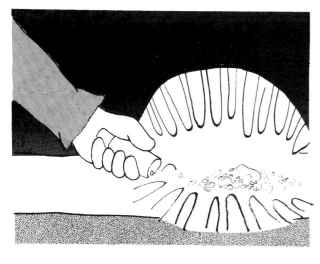

HEY, WHERE YA GOIN'

... GOTTA GO STOKE THE STOVE

...WIFE'S CALLING...

NICE DAY FOR A WALK...

THE KLONDIKE RIVER VALLEY WAS SOON OVERRUN WITH BUSY PROSPECTORS

THIS MINE IS MINE

I CLAIM THIS CLAIM

WHILE THE NEWS OF THE BIG STRIKE SPREAD LIKE WILDFIRE UP & DOWN THE RIVER

GOLD!

GOLD!

OGILVIE

CIRCLE CITY

PAYDIRT!

SOON EVERY MINER IN THE YUKON & ALASKA WAS RUNNING TO THE NEW ELDORADO. QUICKLY THE BEST LAND WAS STAKED BEFORE THE "OUTSIDE" HAD EVEN HEARD THE WORD "KLONDIKE"

ALL NORTHERN MINING TOWNS SOON BECAME GHOST TOWNS

AND AT THE JUNCTION OF THE YUKON & KLONDIKE RIVERS DAWSON WAS BORN

MEANWHILE, ON THE CREEKS, BEDROCK HAD TO BE STRUCK BEFORE ANYONE KNEW THE TRUE VALUE OF THEIR CLAIM

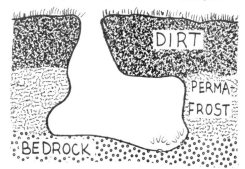

CLARENCE BERRY WAS ONE OF THE FIRST TO HIT IT

BEDROCK!

HEY CLARENCE, HOW'S IT LOOK DOWN THERE?

BETTER...

BETTER WHAT?

BETTER TAKE A LOOK, I THINK WE'RE RICH!

CLARENCE HAD HIT THE PAYSTREAK ON HIS FIRST TRY, CONFIRMING THE KLONDIKE'S RICHES

SO, IN A MATTER OF MONTHS, PREVIOUSLY POOR PROSPECTORS NOW KNEW WEALTH BEYOND THEIR WILDEST DREAMS & EXPECTATIONS

THE LUCKY SWEDE

MONEY & MINES MOVED QUICKLY FROM HAND TO HAND ONCE THE RICH GROUND WAS DISCOVERED, AS THIS STORY ILLUSTRATES. SWEDISH-BORN PROSPECTOR CHARLEY ANDERSON WAS ALMOST BROKE FROM WORKING BARREN MINES. YET IN A MONTH'S TIME HE WOULD BE KNOWN AS "THE LUCKY SWEDE"...

CHARLEY WAS FEELING BLUE & WOUND UP IN A LOCAL SALOON TO TRY & DROWN HIS SORROWS...

THIS CLAIM'S WORTHLESS, WE'VE GOT TO UNLOAD IT.

HOW 'BOUT CHARLEY? HE'S SMASHED!

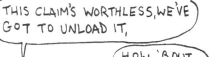

HEY BUDDY, HAVE WE GOT A DEAL FOR YOU...

A VERY VALUABLE CLAIM, WANNA BUY?

UM, (HIC) SURE!

THE NEXT MORNING... OH, MY ACHING HEAD. HEY, WHAT'S THIS?

OH, NO!

WITH THE LAST OF HIS MONEY SUNK IN THE CLAIM, OFF HE WENT TO GIVE IT A TRY...

GOOD LUCK CHARLEY

THANKS I'LL NEED IT

BUT CHARLEY'S LUCK WAS ABOUT TO CHANGE.

JACKPOT!

AND WHAT BECAME OF CHARLEY'S SCAMMERS?

SAY... AREN'T THOSE THE GUYS THAT SOLD YOU THE "BUM" CLAIM?

(HEE, HEE) THAT'S RIGHT

HA HA

HA, HA HA HA HA HA

THE EGG EPISODE

Dawson's early days were marked with both shortages & excesses; salt was worth its weight in gold & eggs were the most expensive item on the menu. Speaking of excess, meet "Swiftwater" Bill Gates:

Swiftwater Bill quickly gained a reputation for his flamboyancy ____

GET THE CARDS GOING BOYS, SKY'S THE LIMIT... AND IF THE ROOF'S IN THE WAY, WHY, TEAR IT OFF!

He had the only white starched collar in town & would take to bed when it was being laundered ____

BETTER THAN BEING SEEN WITHOUT IT!

One day Bill's girlfriend entered a restaurant on the arm of another

!?

YES, I'D LIKE EGGS PLEASE... & YOU DEAR?

ME TOO, PLEASE. I JUST ADORE EGGS!

In a flash Bill ran out and bought EVERY egg in town...

And then, as legend has it, fried & flipped them to a receptive husky audience ____

HA, HA, HA, HA

THE GOLD SHIPS

THE LUCKY SWEDE & SWIFTWATER BILL WERE ONLY 2 OF MANY TO STRIKE IT RICH IN THE EARLY DAYS. AS THE LONG WINTER ENDED & THE SPRING RUNOFF WAS USED TO SEPARATE THE GOLD FROM THE MUD, IMMENSE QUANTITIES OF THE SHINY METAL WERE RETRIEVED

RABBIT CREEK WAS RENAMED BONANZA, & ITS TRIBUTARY, THE RICHEST CREEK OF ALL, WAS KNOWN AS ELDORADO

G'DAY

G'DAY

WITH THE ICE OFF THE YUKON RIVER, BOATS BEGAN TO ARRIVE IN DAWSON, BOATS ORIGINALLY BOUND FOR CIRCLE CITY

HOME IS WHERE THE GOLD IS

10 MONTHS HAD PASSED SINCE THE DISCOVERY & THE OUTSIDE WORLD WAS STILL UNAWARE OF THE KLONDIKE'S WEALTH...

IT WOULD TAKE THE ARRIVAL OF 80 SOURDOUGHS HEADING SOUTH TO TRIGGER THE MASS MOVEMENT KNOWN AS THE KLONDIKE GOLD RUSH. SO, ON BOARD 2 DECREPIT OCEAN-FARING VESSELS CLIMBED THE RAGGED PROSPECTORS. ONCE DIRT-POOR, THEY NOW HURRIED HOME TO FAMILY & FRIENDS...

...COLLECTIVELY POSSESSING OVER 3 TONS OF GOLD...

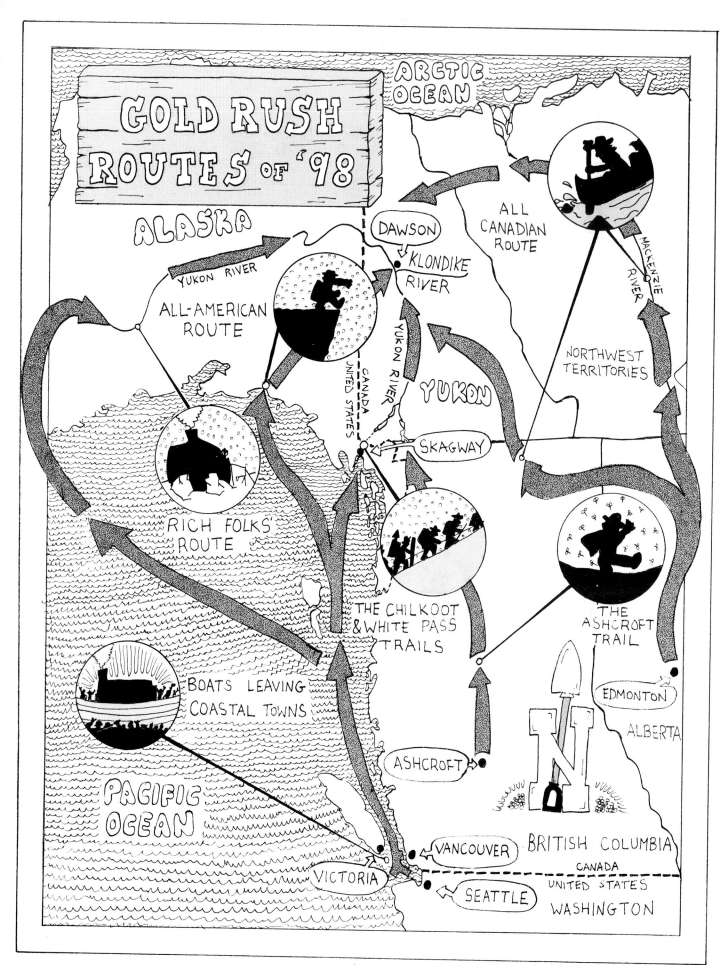

BOUND FOR GLORY

IT IS ESTIMATED THAT OVER 1,000,000 PEOPLE LAID PLANS TO GO TO THE KLONDIKE, WITH MORE THAN 100,000 ACTUALLY SETTING OUT. FOR MANY THIS OPTIMISM WOULD TURN TO DESPAIR BEFORE LONG. BUT AT THE TIME ONLY ONE THING MATTERED: GET TO THE GOLD!

DOCTORS, LAWYERS & POLICEMEN BOARDED SHIPS KLONDIKE-BOUND...

RUBBING SHOULDERS WITH TRANSIENTS, EX-CONS & GAMBLERS.

MEN & WOMEN OF ALL AGES & OCCUPATIONS WENT...

ALEA JACTA EST

AND ANIMALS OF ALL SHAPES & SIZES.

COMING ON BOARD?

THANKS, ILL FLY

PANDEMONIUM REIGNED IN SEATTLE, WHERE OVER 10,000 LEFT THEIR JOBS, INCLUDING THE MAYOR...

HOLD MY CALLS, I'M OFF TO THE KLONDIKE!

THE CANADIAN GOVERNMENT QUICKLY SENT UP A LEGION OF MOUNTIES TO REINFORCE THOSE ALREADY STATIONED

AND OF COURSE, THE NEWS OF THE STRIKE REACHED THE EARS OF ADVENTURERS AROUND THE WORLD.

J'ADORE L'OR!

YA, VE GO TO KLONDIKE TOO!

16

GOODS & SERVICES

© OF THE TENS OF THOUSANDS HEADING NORTH PRECIOUS FEW KNEW THE FIRST THING ABOUT MINING. COASTAL TOWNS LIKE SEATTLE, VICTORIA, SAN FRANCISCO & VANCOUVER WERE SWAMPED WITH DEPARTING GOLD SEEKERS & DIME-A-DOZEN SALESMEN.

I'M GOING THIS SPRING

Ⓐ NYTHING WITH THE NAME "KLONDIKE" ON IT WAS A SURE SELL

OFFICIAL KLONDIKE SOCKS & SHOES

YUKON STOVES HERE

CREAM OF KLONDIKE SOUP

Ⓐ BSURD SERVICES LIKE "THE TRANS-ALASKA GOPHER COMPANY" & "KLONDIKE CLAIRVOYANCE" BEGAN BUSINESS.

...TRAINED GOPHERS, THEY DIG FOR GOLD WHILE YOU GET RICH!

I SEE...... GOLD! IN YOUR NEAR FUTURE...

I'M SOLD!

YOU'RE HIRED

Ⓐ NUMBER OF TRANSPORTATION SCHEMES WERE LAUNCHED USING "BOATSLEDS"...

KLONDIKE...

...OR BUST

CRACK

BALLOON'S...

ANY GOLD ON THE MOON?

YOU'RE GOING TO BIKE TO THE KLONDIKE?

& BICYCLES

HEY, IT'S ALL CYCLE-LOGICAL

Ⓣ O MAKE THINGS MORE CONFUSING, THERE WASN'T JUST ONE ROUTE TO THE GOLD FIELDS, THERE WERE MANY

ALL-AMERICAN ROUTE, THE ONLY WAY

EDMONTON! GATEWAY TO THE YUKON

CLIMB THE CHILKOOT PASS; START IN SEATTLE

Ⓢ O, ARMED WITH MISINFORMATION & FAULTY GOODS, THE GREAT ARMY OF GOLD SEEKERS GOT UNDER WAY

HEY! WHAT'S THAT?

JUST BOUGHT IT! THE NEW KLONDIKE X-RAY MACHINE..DETECTS GOLD IN STREAMS

WOW! YOU'LL BE RICH!

17

KLONDIKE OR BUST

THE EXCITEMENT & URGENCY OF THE RUSH SENT MANY SCRAMBLING FOR TRANSPORTATION. SHIPS LONG CONDEMNED WERE PULLED OUT OF THE BONEYARDS & PUT INTO SERVICE... REGARDLESS OF CONDITION

HO! FOR THE KLONDIKE!

SOME BOATS OVERLOADED,

CHUG-A CHUG-A

SOME LEAKED,

SOME CAUGHT FIRE,

UM... CAPTAIN...

WHAT NOW?

AND OTHERS...WELL...

BOOM

BUT THE MAJORITY KEPT GOING...

THE SPIRITS OF THE PASSENGERS SLIGHTLY DAMPENED

SIGH

HO! FOR THE ✱☠✦⚡✦☺◎ KLONDIKE

RICH FOLKS' ROUTE

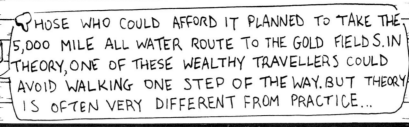

Those who could afford it planned to take the 5,000 mile all water route to the gold fields. In theory, one of these wealthy travellers could avoid walking one step of the way. But theory is often very different from practice...

Passengers had to endure everything from overcrowded boats to...

Questionable quarters.

Many made it to the Yukon River...

Only to watch it freeze in around them.

Almost 3,000 people were therefore locked in for a sub-zero winter in the icy northland

19

ALL-AMERICAN ROUTE

OF THE MANY ROUTES TO THE KLONDIKE, THIS JOURNEY ACROSS THE FROZEN ALASKAN MOUNTAINS WAS PERHAPS THE MOST DANGEROUS. THE FACT THAT SO MANY CHOSE IT ILLUSTRATES THE FOOLISHNESS THAT WAS INHERENT IN GOLD FEVER...

THOUSANDS WERE DUMPED ON THE SOUTHERN COAST OF ALASKA, HOME OF NORTH AMERICA'S LARGEST MOUNTAINS...

UM... I THINK I LEFT MY WATER RUNNING AT HOME...

SHADDUP, WE'RE GOING OVER

AMAZINGLY, SOME 3,500 ACTUALLY MADE IT TO THE TOP OF VALDEZ GLACIER...

REMEMBER! NUGGETS AS **BIG** AS BIRD'S EGGS.

AND MOVED ACROSS THE ICEFIELDS,

ALL THE TIME DEALING WITH SNOWBLINDNESS...

ICY CREVASSES...

UM... HARRY...

WHAT?

AND THE OBLIGATORY

AVALANCHE!

RUMBLE RUMBLE

BOOM

ONLY ABOUT 20 PEOPLE MADE IT TO DAWSON. THOSE WHO RETREATED WERE A LITTLE, SHALL WE SAY... TRAUMATIZED!

...AND THEN THE SNOWBEAST JUMPED ON JOHN'S BACK...

...CRUSHING HIM INSTANTLY!

PRESS

THE ASHCROFT TRAIL

This trail, sometimes known as "The Spectral Trail," followed an old mining route through the heart of British Columbia. Besides the incredible distance involved, travelling **BY FOOT** was the only way to cross this sea of mud, bugs & despair

Thousands underestimated the difficulty of this trail...

I'm off to strike it rich!

OK, dear, but be home for Christmas

And naively trusted self-serving salesmen.

...Best trail, 2 months & you'll be ankle deep in gold nuggets...

SUPPLIES FOR SALE

DAWSON: 1200 M

GREAT!

BEANS

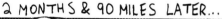

2 months & 90 miles later...

For those that took this route anything that could go wrong...

OUCH, OUCH

DID go wrong.

OUCH, OUCH, OUCH OUCH!

The trail was littered with the discarded gear of discouraged stampeders...

...ever feel like you were being watched?

As well as the odd suicide note...

CARE TO GO/BACK NOW?

BURY ME HERE WHERE I FAILED

ALL-CANADIAN ROUTE

The farming community of Edmonton appealed to Canadian & British patriotism by advertising "The All-Canadian Route" to the gold fields. But as time would prove the 2 trails departing Edmonton were amongst the most difficult of all...

The first route traversed over 1,500 miles of treacherous terrain

6 WEEKS TILL THE GOLD...

FORTUNE AWAITS US!

The trail grew gradually smaller & smaller until it disappeared completely

HEY! WHAT'S THAT SAY?

DUE NORTH TO DAWSON: STARVATION & DEATH; DUE SOUTH: HOME SWEET HOME & A WARM BED...

NEEDLESS TO SAY, MOST TURNED BACK

AND DESTRUCTION CITY.

The stampeders often named the obstacles they passed appropriate names..

The second route followed the Mackenzie River system for 2,500 miles.

LIKE BOILER RAPIDS

DEVIL'S PORTAGE

8 MILES

Amazingly, over 2/3 of those who tried this route made it... but it would take them 2 years to do it!

But the snow had arrived & all over the north thousands were trapped in for the long winter.

CAN YOU SAY FROZEN TOES?

CAN YOU SAY TEPID BOREDOM?

Meanwhile, amongst Dawson's population of 6,000, panic was beginning to set in...

FLEE! WHILE YOU STILL CAN!

GRIM PROSPECTS

AMAZINGLY, ADEQUATE SUPPLIES HAD FAILED TO REACH DAWSON BEFORE FREEZE-UP. THE PROSPECT OF SLOWLY STARVING IN THIS HARSH CLIMATE SENT OVER A THOUSAND PEOPLE FLEEING THE COVETED GOLD CITY...

WITH THE ICE ALREADY FILLING THE RIVER, 150 BOATS DEPARTED...

BUT THEIR ESCAPE WOULD BE SHORT-LIVED.

I THINK MY NOSE IS FROZE

MOST RETURNED & WOULD WHILE AWAY THE WINTER MONTHS MINING...

GRUMBLE GRUMBLE

GAMBLING & DANCING. GOLD BECAME ALMOST WORTHLESS & MOVED QUICKLY FROM HAND TO HAND

THIS ROUND'S ON ME!

...& ANOTHER 4 OUNCES ON BLACK

...THAT IS UNTIL A FIRE WIPED OUT MOST OF THE BUSINESS SECTION.

YET, DESPITE THE PROBLEMS IN DAWSON CITY, VAST HORDES OF GOLD SEEKERS WERE USING THEIR EVERY RESOURCE TO GET THERE, WHICH BRINGS US TO SKAGWAY & THE ONLY VIABLE ROUTE TO THE KLONDIKE.

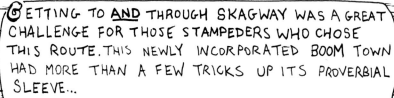

FIRST IMPRESSIONS

Getting to **AND** through Skagway was a great challenge for those stampeders who chose this route. This newly incorporated boom town had more than a few tricks up its proverbial sleeve...

After several tortuous weeks at sea, the stampeders finally reached the Alaskan town

LAND HO!

For many, docking at Skagway was a rather taxing experience as they were quickly introduced to ¼ mile docks...

Icy wharves...

SPLASH

High tides...

& some of the local scammers.

LIFE IN SKAGWAY

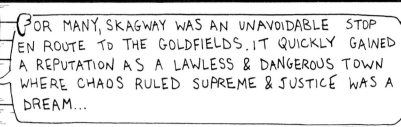

FOR MANY, SKAGWAY WAS AN UNAVOIDABLE STOP EN ROUTE TO THE GOLDFIELDS. IT QUICKLY GAINED A REPUTATION AS A LAWLESS & DANGEROUS TOWN WHERE CHAOS RULED SUPREME & JUSTICE WAS A DREAM...

THIS BOOM TOWN, SOMETIMES KNOWN AS "THE WORST HELLHOLE ON EARTH" HELD A DISPROPORTIONATE NUMBER OF GAMBLERS, GOONS & GUNSLINGERS...

"SOAPY SMITH" CONTROLLED THE CRIMINAL ELEMENT IN TOWN

HIS GANG OF CARDSHARKS & CON MEN CHEATED MANY STAMPEDERS OUT OF THEIR MONEY & GOODS, EFFECTIVELY KNOCKING THEM OUT OF THE RACE.

BUT FOR THOSE WHO MADE IT THROUGH SKAGWAY UNSCATHED THESE TRIALS WERE BUT A SAMPLE OF WHAT WAS TO COME...

THE CHILKOOT PASS

CHAPTER 3

"Never will I forget it, there on the mountain face,
Antlike, men with their burdens, clinging in icy space;
Dogged, determined and dauntless, cruel and callous and cold,
Cursing, blaspheming, reviling, and always that battlecry—"Gold"

"The trail of '98"
Robert Service

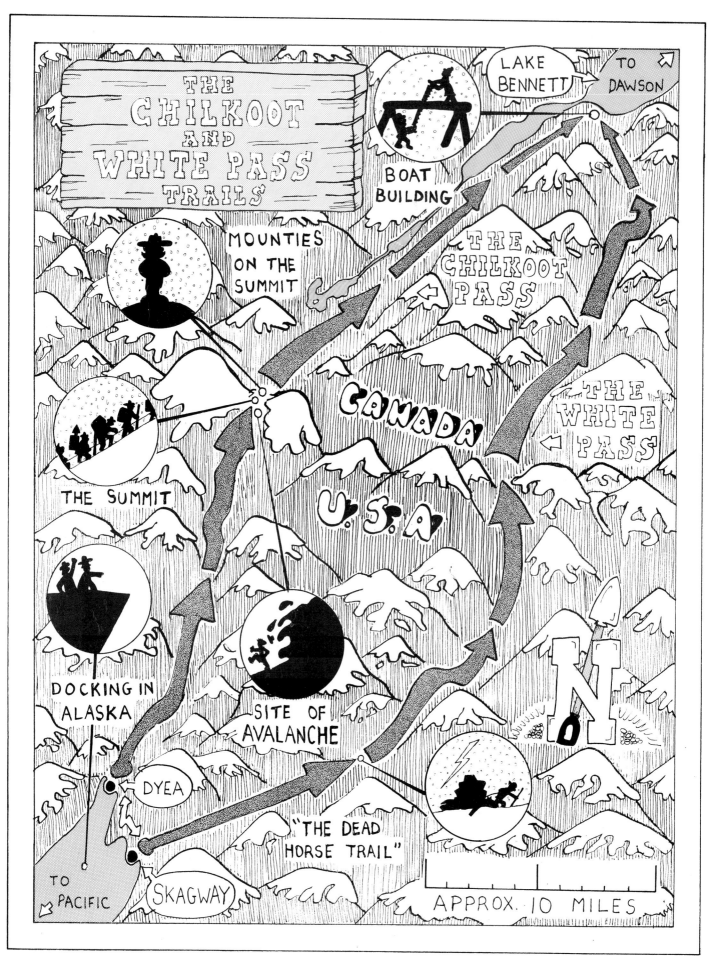

TWO TRAILS

DAWSON WAS GOING THROUGH ITS SECOND WINTER OF SHORTAGES, SO THE MOUNTIES' STATIONED ON THE SUMMITS PASSED A NEW LAW: ANYONE ENTERING CANADA MUST POSSESS ADEQUATE SUPPLIES FOR A YEAR IN THE NORTHLAND...OR BE DENIED ENTRY!

THOSE LUCKY ENOUGH TO MAKE IT THROUGH SKAGWAY WITH GEAR INTACT SET OFF FOR THE WHITE PASS OR THE CHILKOOT PASS

THIEF!

BANG

CRASH

HELP

AND IN NEARBY DYEA THOUSANDS MORE DISEMBARKED FOR THE TRAILS

BUT, ALAS, SKAGWAY'S INFLUENCE WAS STILL FELT AS SOAPY'S GANG WORKED THEIR "TRADE" ALONG THE SNOWY PASSES

CHILKOOT PASS   WHITE PASS

BOTH TRAILS OFFERED ALMOST INSURMOUNTABLE CHALLENGES, BUT FIRST, A LOOK AT THE WHITE PASS...

THE WHITE PASS

This trail, though not too long, was in very poor shape & it would take months to relay goods the distance. Scores of eager gold seekers were ill-prepared for the trauma they were about to experience...

The beginning of the trail was deceptively easy...

JUST LIKE A SUNDAY WALK...

GULP: DON'T SPEAK TOO SOON

WHEEZE
GRUNT
GROAN
OUCH!

To complete this 46 mile trail they had first to conquer the cliffs of Devil's Hill,

The jagged peaks of Porcupine Hill,

And the mudholes of Summit Hill.

Thousands snaked through the pass, rarely moving faster than a snail's crawl.

The trail was quickly dubbed "The Dead Horse Trail" for of the 3,000 horses to travel it scarcely one survived

SIGH: NO AMOUNT OF GOLD IS WORTH **THIS**!

In addition to all the natural obstacles, stampeders had to watch out for soapy smith's gang of cardsharks & thugs...

CARE TO JOIN ME FOR A GAME OF POKER?

SURE, WHAT HAVE I GOT TO LOSE?

THE APPROACH

OF THE MANY TRAILS TO THE KLONDIKE THIS ONE PROVED TO BE THE BEST. SO, IN THE DEAD OF WINTER, 1898, OVER 22,000 PEOPLE WOULD CROSS THE LITTLE NOTCH IN THE MOUNTAINS KNOWN AS...

THE CHILKOOT PASS!

MILLIONS OF TONS OF GOODS HAD TO BE TRANSPORTED OVER THE TRAIL. NATIVE PACKERS WERE HIRED & ANIMALS UTILIZED.

PHOTOGRAPHER ERIC HEGG FOLLOWED THE RUSH, AIDED BY HIS MOST UNUSUAL SLED TEAM.

IN FACT ANY ANIMAL THAT COULD PULL WAS EMPLOYED.

HO, HO, HO FOR THE KLONDIKE

BUT NO ANIMAL, SAVE HUMAN, COULD CLIMB THE DREADED SUMMIT!

!

31

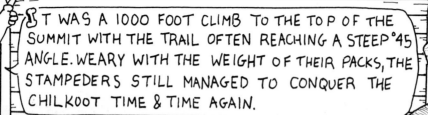

OVER THE TOP

IT WAS A 1000 FOOT CLIMB TO THE TOP OF THE SUMMIT WITH THE TRAIL OFTEN REACHING A STEEP 45° ANGLE. WEARY WITH THE WEIGHT OF THEIR PACKS, THE STAMPEDERS STILL MANAGED TO CONQUER THE CHILKOOT TIME & TIME AGAIN.

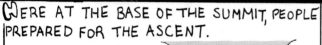

HERE AT THE BASE OF THE SUMMIT, PEOPLE PREPARED FOR THE ASCENT.

50 POUNDS WAS THE AVERAGE WEIGHT OF A LOAD, WITH THE RECORD OF 350 POUNDS SET BY ONE OF THE NATIVE PACKERS.

NEXT TIME WE HIRE HIM

IT TOOK ON AVERAGE 40 TRIPS UP THIS ICY MOUNTAINSIDE TO MOVE ONE'S GEAR, EACH CLIMB TAKING UP TO 6 HOURS

THE TRIP DOWN TO THE BASE HOWEVER TOOK BUT A FEW MINUTES

YEE-HAA

MEET THE MOUNTIES

THE U.S.-CANADA BORDER WAS IN DISPUTE PRIOR TO THE GOLDRUSH, BUT A BRIGADE OF MOUNTIES ARMED WITH MAXIM GUNS QUICKLY SETTLED IT. PERCHED ON THIS PRECIPITOUS POINT THEY ENDURED MANY PRIVATIONS IN THE NAME OF LAW & ORDER.

THEIR MAIN DUTY WAS TO ENSURE THAT EVERYONE HAD ADEQUATE SUPPLIES TO SURVIVE FOR A YEAR IN THIS HARSH CLIMATE.

SAM STEELE (A.K.A. "THE LION OF THE YUKON") KEPT CONTROL AMIDST THIS CHAOS,

AND AN AVERAGE TEMPERATURE OF -40°F!

HACK
WHEEZE..

EVEN DURING FREQUENT WHITEOUTS...

JOE! WHERE ARE YOU?

NO CLUE

EVEN IN THE FACE OF VIOLENCE.

STEELE & HIS MOUNTIES ALSO KEPT UNDESIRABLES LIKE SOAPY'S GANG OUT OF THE COUNTRY,

THEY ALWAYS GET THEIR MAN

...AND WHAT IF I DECIDE TO SHOOT MY WAY INTO CANADA!?!

HERE'S A GUN, FIND OUT FOR YOURSELF.

AVALANCHE!

The mountain passes that the stampeders traversed were both stunningly beautiful & unpredictably dangerous. A flash flood had frightened many but it paled in comparison to... **THE AVALANCHE!**

Over 70 feet of snow fell on the Chilkoot that winter, burying people's gear almost instantly

COULD HAVE SWORN I LEFT IT RIGHT HERE!

PROBABLY STILL THERE, START DIGGIN'

During one especially snowy week the native packers refused to move, but many ignored their warnings...

NO GO!

BAH

Until on April 3, 1898, the inevitable happened

RUMBLE

BOOM!

RUMBLE

RUN FOR YOUR LIVES!

Many came to the rescue & worked day & night pulling the victims from the snow,

Alas, for over 60, it was too late

But the snow...er...show must go on...

DID YOU HEAR SOMETHING?

SHHHHHH!

RUMBLE RUMBLE

TO BUILD A BOAT...

BY EARLY SPRING MOST OF THE STAMPEDERS HAD SUCCESSFULLY MOVED THEIR GOODS OVER THE PASSES & REACHED LAKE BENNETT, WHERE THEY FRANTICALLY WORKED ON BOATS TO TAKE THEM DOWN THE YUKON RIVER TO THE GOLDFIELDS

BOATBUILDING WAS, AT BEST, AN ARDUOUS TASK

FIRST TREES WERE FELLED,

AND THEN WHIPSAWED.

HEY! WATCH IT!

WATCH WHAT?

THIS!

THE WHIPSAWING CAUSED MANY A PARTNERSHIP TO DISSOLVE, MUTUAL GOODS BEING DIVIDED IN HALF...LITERALLY!

DESPITE THE BICKERING, A VERITABLE NAVY WAS BEING BUILT. AMONGST THESE CRAFTS MOVED THE MOUNTIES, ENSURING SAFETY STANDARDS.

EVER BUILD A BOAT BEFORE?

NO, BUT I BUILT A BOOKSHELF ONCE!

NO KIDDING

THE CRAZY ARMADA

BY SPRING OVER 7,000 "VESSELS" WERE READY TO TRAVERSE THE FRIGID WATERS OF THE YUKON RIVER. EVERY CONCEIVABLE TYPE OF BOAT WAS BUILT, FROM SCOWS & SKIFFS TO KAYAKS & CATAMARANS...

EAGERLY THEY WAITED UNTIL...

THAR' GOES THE ICE!

CRACK

AND THE RACE WAS ON!

HO! FOR THE KLONDIKE

DAWSON OR BUST!

HEY, YOUR BOAT LOOKS JUST LIKE A COFFIN!

I KNOW. IT **IS** A COFFIN

AND AS THE FIRST DAY ENDED...

HEY RAY LET'S CALL IT A DAY

SURE JAY SOUNDS OK

THE FLEET RELAXED KNOWING THAT THEIR GOAL WAS BUT A BOATRIDE AWAY...

THERE'S GOLD IN THEM HILLS

THERE'S GOLD IN THEM HILLS

WHITEWATER!

However, relaxation had to wait, for it was a 2 week haul into Dawson with more challenges awaiting. Hastily-built craft & weather-beaten gold seekers had yet to face... WHITEWATER!

DO YOU HEAR SOMETHING JAKE?

IT'S WHAT?

OH MY GOD, IT'S... IT'S...

GURGLE GURGLE

IT'S...

RAPIDS!

A few hundred decided to run the rapids, with disastrous results!

Afraid to go any further, thousands of ships were bottlenecked at the start of the rapids. Enter Sam Steele:

SOME SAY THE MOUNTIES MAKE THE LAWS UP AS THEY GO & I SHALL DO SO NOW...

With the mounties' help the fleet was safely shuttled through

And so the race continued with many more boats joining in from the Yukon River's myriad tributaries...

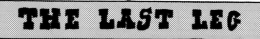

THE LAST LEG

For the rest of the journey, where rapids were found, mounties were also present. The only danger remaining was the flying temper of an irate partner gone mad from the elements...

Like the scorching sun...

And swarming skitters.

ARRGHH!

BUZZZZZZZ

BZZZZZZZ

But as the days passed, anticipation grew as they approached...

DAWSON!

THE CITY OF GOLD!

CHAPTER 4

BOOMTOWN!

And I'll strike it, yes, I'll strike it; I've a hunch I cannot fail;
I've a vision, I've a prompting, I've a call;
I hear the hoarse stampeding of an army on my trail,
To the last, the greatest gold camp of them all.

"The Prospector"
Robert Service

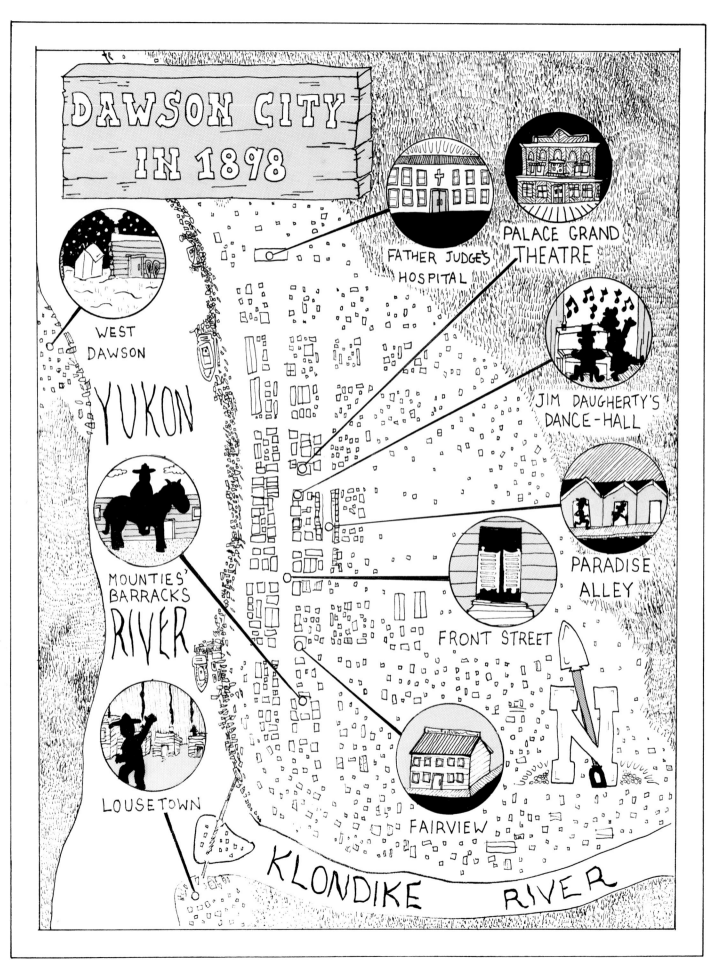

THE FLEET ARRIVES

THE RESIDENTS OF DAWSON WERE OVERJOYED AS THE FIRST WAVE OF STAMPEDERS HIT TOWN. IT HAD BEEN A LONG, HUNGRY WINTER & THE NEW ARRIVALS MEANT SUPPLIES, ENTERTAINMENT & WHO KNOWS WHAT ELSE!

THE MELTING OF THE SPRING ICE HAD FLOODED DAWSON'S MAIN STRIP...

BUT THAT HARDLY DAZED THE EXUBERANT STAMPEDERS

END OF THE RAINBOW

HOWEVER, THERE WASN'T MUCH GOLD TO BRING ON, FOR MOST OF THE RICH GROUND HAD BEEN STAKED. THOSE WHO HAD ANTICIPATED SHORTAGES & LUGGED LOADS OF GOODS ALONG, WOULD BE THE REAL WINNERS OF THE RACE TO DAWSON.

A MAN DOCKING WITH A BOATFUL OF KITTENS WAS ABLE TO SELL THEM FOR AN OUNCE OF GOLD APIECE.

ANOTHER, LOADED WITH THE LATEST FASHIONS, CLEARED AN AMAZING PROFIT.

IT'S YOU

A POUND OF NAILS FETCHED HALF AN OUNCE OF GOLD...

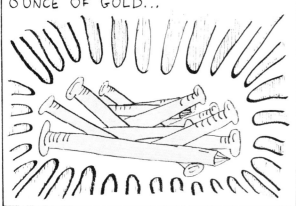

AND A RELATIVELY RECENT NEWSPAPER, THOUGH SOAKED IN BACON FAT, GATHERED A FULL OUNCE.

SPANISH WAR BEGINS! QUEEN'S FINE!! SOMETHING ABOUT US IN HERE TOO...

AND THEN THERE WAS THE ARRIVAL OF THE FIRST FRESH DAIRY PRODUCTS...

DO I HEAR FOUR?

FOUR DOLLARS FOR THE FIRST EGG LAID IN DAWSON?

FIVE!

PARIS OF THE NORTH

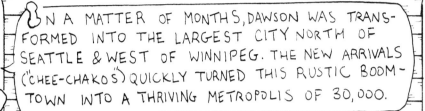

IN A MATTER OF MONTHS, DAWSON WAS TRANSFORMED INTO THE LARGEST CITY NORTH OF SEATTLE & WEST OF WINNIPEG. THE NEW ARRIVALS ("CHEE-CHAKOS") QUICKLY TURNED THIS RUSTIC BOOM-TOWN INTO A THRIVING METROPOLIS OF 30,000.

AS THE FLOOD SUBSIDED THE CITY OF GOLD TURNED INTO THE CITY OF MUD—

UNBELIEVABLE COLD, SHORTAGES & STARVATION, FIRE, FLOOD & NOW KNEE-DEEP MUD...

IT'S A SADIST'S PARADISE

MANY WHO HAD DISSOLVED THEIR PARTNERSHIPS EN ROUTE RE-UNITED. ...AND THAT TIME THE WHOLE RAFT CAME APART...

AND WE BOTH WENT SWIMMING WITH THE SALMON

NEWSPAPERS LIKE "THE KLONDIKE NUGGET" & "THE MIDNIGHT SUN" OPENED SHOP.

RUMOUR OF GOLD ON DOMINION CREEK!

CLICK CLICK CLICK

"PARADISE ALLEY" WITH ITS HOUSES OF ILL REPUTE, FLOURISHED.

...IN THE MOOD FOR A LITTLE HORIZONTAL ENTERTAINMENT?

IN FACT, IN CONTRAST TO THE PREVIOUS WINTER **ANYTHING** COULD NOW BE PURCHASED...

TODAY'S SPECIALS: LOBSTER & CAVIAR...

PHONE'S FOR YOU, FRANK

THIS EVENING'S PERFORMANCE OF CAMILLE. STARS...

AVOCADOS & RUTABAGAS

GOLD FILLINGS?

YUP, REAL MAMMOTH TUSKS

?

45

ECCENTRICS & ENTREPRENEURS

For months after the river cleared, hordes of humans poured on to the banks of the Gold City. Since only those resourceful & lucky enough had completed the quest, the city soon became a mosaic of colorful diversity

Unique nicknames were the norm...

HI! I'M "TWO-STEP" LOUIE

THEY CALL ME BILLY THE HORSE

LOOK OVER THERE! IT'S SILENT SAM...

As an introduction to the locals will reveal:

TO EULOGIZE OR NOT TO EULOGIZE?

Captain Jack Crawford "Poet-Scout of the Sierras", who would compose many a poem about the Golden City.

THE LORD'S WORK IS NEVER DONE...

Father William Judge, who had the first church & hospital built, was known as "The Saint of Dawson" for his benevolence in a time of greed & excess.

TO RAISE MY IRE...

IS TO COURT CALAMITY!

Sharp-shooting Calamity Jane, who once rubbed shoulders with Wild Bill Hickok, was in town...

GREATEST THRILL OF MY LIFE!

And there was "Coatless Curly," who had run the rapids lashed to his boat (without a coat of course).

There are two legendary figures of the Stampede, however, who deserve special attention...

ARIZONA CHARLIE MEADOWS

Arizona Charlie was a sharpshooting scout & entrepreneur from the old wild west shows. Well, the west was no longer wild so Charlie decided to make his fortune by following the final frontier...

En route to Dawson, Charlie had opened his portable bar & casino...

BEST WHISKEY ON THE CHILKOOT, & THE FINEST GAMBLING, TO BOOT.

Until a flash flood closed him down.

LAST CALL FOLKS!

WHOOSH

So Charlie turned to profiting from his sharp shooting skills

BANG!

Soon after arriving in Dawson, Charlie had the famous Palace Grand Theatre built.

Inside, plays were the norm, as was Charlie's sharp-shooting

BANG

And they say he never missed his mark

WELL, ALMOST NEVER..

BELINDA'S BAR

ANOTHER AMAZING SUCCESS STORY IS THAT OF AN ENTERPRISING WOMAN BY THE NAME OF BELINDA MULRONEY. SHE HAD FLOATED INTO DAWSON SHORTLY AFTER THE RUSH BEGAN WITH HUNDREDS OF HOT WATER BOTTLES & A GRAND PLAN...

UPON ARRIVING IN DAWSON, SHE TOSSED HER LAST 50 CENT PIECE INTO THE RIVER, EXCLAIMING:

THERE IT IS! THE CITY OF GOLD! I'LL NEVER NEED SUCH SMALL CHANGE AGAIN

PLINK

SHE QUICKLY REALIZED A 600% PROFIT FROM HER GOODS & BEGAN TO SCOUT FOR A CHOICE SITE ON WHICH TO SET UP HER DREAM ROADHOUSE.

HMMMM... TOO MUCH COMPETITION...

SALOON HOT

BELINDA STRATEGICALLY CHOSE THE JUNCTION OF THE 2 RICHEST CREEKS (10 MILES FROM DAWSON) & BEGAN CONSTRUCTION...

CAN'T YOU SEE IT JERRY? THE BEST BAR IN THE KLONDIKE, BAR NONE

BANG BANG GROAN

ZZZZ

DESPITE THE LACK OF SUPPORT.

YOU CAN'T BUILD HERE, EVERYONE GOES TO TOWN TO DRINK

OH, YEAH? WATCH ME!

1 MONTH LATER BELINDA WAS RUNNING A BOOMING BUSINESS.

3 CHEERS FOR BELINDA!

C'MON IN FOLKS

THE MAGNET

AND 3 CHEERS FOR JERRY!

HMMM.. NEVER THOUGHT I'D SEE YOU IN HERE...

WELL..UM...YA KNOW...

GRAND FORKS

BELINDA WAS IN AN IDEAL SPOT FOR PICKING UP MINING GOSSIP & IN NO TIME OWNED HALF A DOZEN CLAIMS. MEANWHILE HER WATERING HOLE BECAME SO POPULAR THAT A TOWN GREW UP AROUND IT.

APPROPRIATELY NAMED GRAND FORKS, IT TOOK ONLY A FEW MONTHS FOR THE POPULATION TO REACH 10,000.

PICKS, PACKS & POKES FOR SALE

WOW! LOOK AT THE SIZE OF THAT NUGGET

DRINKS ON ME!

AROUND TOWN STROLLED A PROUD BELINDA MULRONEY, WITH JERRY THE MULE & NERO, HER HUGE SAINT BERNARD,

IT WOULD BE THIS DOG THAT A YOUNG AUTHOR NAMED JACK LONDON WOULD MODEL HIS CANINE HERO "BUCK" AFTER IN HIS UPCOMING BOOK CALL OF THE WILD.

ONE HOSTELRY, HOWEVER, WAS NOT ENOUGH FOR THIS AMBITIOUS WOMAN, SO SHE HAD THE RENOWNED "FAIRVIEW" BUILT IN DAWSON

FAMOUS FOR ITS TURKISH BATHS & STEAM-HEATED ROOMS, IT HAD ONLY 1 REAL FLAW... PAPER-THIN WALLS

LA LA LA!

SIGH

MEANWHILE IN SKAGWAY, THINGS WERE GOING FROM BAD TO ABYSMAL...

SOAPY'S REIGN

ⒽUNDREDS OF GOLD SEEKERS STILL PASSED THROUGH SKAGWAY DAILY & INTO THE WAITING ARMS OF JEFFERSON "SOAPY" SMITH & HIS MINIONS. FEW TOWNS IN HISTORY HAVE BEEN SO COMPLETELY DOMINATED BY ORGANIZED CRIME...

ⓈOAPY HAD ARRIVED IN SKAGWAY WITH A SMALL GANG OF HANDPICKED CON MEN

BUT IN MONTHS UPON ARRIVING, HIS CONTROL EXTENDED TO OVER 300 CARDSHARKS & THUGS.

WELCOME TO SKAGWAY..

TAX TIME

ⒽIS MOST FAMOUS VENUE FOR RIP-OFFS WAS HIS OYSTER PARLOUR, FOOD UP FRONT & "SURE-THING" GAMES OUT BACK.

THIS LOOKS LIKE A NICE PLACE

THIEVES!

JEFF SMITH'S PARLOUR

ⓄTHER "ESTABLISHMENTS" INCLUDED AN INFORMATION BUREAU...

HOW MUCH MONEY DO YOU HAVE & WHAT ARE YOUR PLANS ?

WINK

AND A FAKE TELEGRAPH OFFICE. NEEDLESS TO SAY, FEW STAMPEDERS LEFT THESE PLACES WITH THEIR MONEY.

ⓈOAPY HIMSELF NEVER TOOK PART IN THE SCAMS, BUT INSTEAD, GAVE EVERY APPEARANCE OF BEING A PUBLIC BENEFACTOR

PATRIOTIC AMERICANS...

LET US DECLARE TODAY OFFICIAL ADOPT-A-DOG DAY...

RED ONION

50

ENTER BILL REID...

§KAGWAY'S LAW-ABIDING CITIZENS WERE SPLIT ON THEIR OPINIONS OF SOAPY, BUT AS HIS FACADE BEGAN TO CHIP, THEY STARTED TO TIRE OF HIM & HIS UNSCRUPULOUS GANG'S EXPLOITS. IT WOULD TAKE ONE BRAVE SOUL TO TIP THE SCALES...

§OAPY BECAME INCREASINGLY INVOLVED WITH CHARITIES (THE MONEY RAISED OFTEN ENDING UP IN HIS POCKETS)..

WHILE HIS GANG SPUN OUT OF CONTROL

HEY BUDDY, WANNA PLAY A GAME?

WHA...!?

HEY! TURN ON THE LIGHTS

BOOM

OUCH!

I GOT IT

CRASH

BANG

SWINE! THIEVING JACKALS!

THIS HAS GOT TO STOP!

HA HA HA

ALL THIS THIEVERY IS AFFECTING BUSINESS

§NTER BILL REID: ...MEETING TONIGHT AT THE WHARF. IT'S TIME FOR SOAPY & HIS GANG TO LEAVE TOWN

OK BILL, I'LL SPREAD THE WORD...

BOSS! THE TOWN IS TURNING AGAINST YOU

WHAT! I'LL GO SETTLE THIS ONCE AND FOR ALL

§S SOAPY STORMED OUT HE BUMPED INTO BILL REID... SMITH, IF YOU DON'T STOP YOUR SWINDLING THERE'S GOING TO BE TROUBLE!

TROUBLE'S WHAT I'M AFTER! GO GET YOUR GUN

SHOOTOUT AT THE DOCK

REID RAN TO GET HIS GUN, BUT ON HIS RETURN SOAPY WAS GONE. SMITH, NOW HALF-DRUNK & ARMED TO THE TEETH, HEARD WORD OF THE MEETING AT THE WHARF & QUICKLY PROCEEDED DOWN THERE...

LET'S SEE SOME IDENTIFICATION PLEASE

HEY REID, HERE COMES SOAPY!

YOU CAN'T GO DOWN THERE SOAPY...

I SHOULD HAVE GOTTEN RID OF YOU LONG AGO

BANG

BANG! BANG

SOAPY WAS A GONER; REID WOULD FOLLOW 12 DAYS LATER.

AAAAHHH!

!

!

ONE OF THE WHARF GUARDS QUICKLY SEIZED CONTROL OF THE SITUATION.

ANYONE IN SOAPY'S GANG BETTER GIT!

WITH THEIR LEADER FALLEN, THE GANG WAS HASTILY CHASED OUT OF TOWN BY A MOB OF LOCALS. SKAGWAY WAS FREE!

BANG!

CELEBRATION DAY

BACK IN DAWSON, MOST OF THE STAMPEDERS HAD ARRIVED AT THEIR GOAL. HAVING CONQUERED THE IMMENSE ODDS AGAINST THEM, IT SEEMED THAT A CELEBRATION WORTHY OF "THE WORLD'S GREATEST GOLD RUSH TOWN" WAS IN ORDER...

THE MINERS CRAWLED OUT OF THEIR MUDDY SHAFTS...

MIXING WITH THE MASSES OF NEWCOMERS

AT ONE MINUTE PAST MIDNIGHT, JULY 4, 1898, A SHOT RANG OUT, SIGNALLING THE START OF THE SOIRÉE

ALL NIGHT LONG & INTO THE NEXT DAY THE PARTY RAGED, SENDING SOME 400 PANICKED DOGS SWIMMING ACROSS THE YUKON RIVER. FOR 12 MONTHS THIS CITY WOULD BE THE SITE OF DECADENCE, DEBAUCHERY & UNPARALLELED EXCITEMENT

BUT, AS IS THE NATURE OF BOOM TOWNS, ITS TIME WAS LIMITED...

CHAPTER 5

ONE GOLDEN YEAR

You'd follow it in hunger, you'd follow it in cold;
You'd follow it in solitude and pain;
And when you're stiff and battered down let someone
whisper "Gold",
You're lief to rise and follow it again.

"The Prospector"
Robert Service

"GOING ON A SPREE"

During Dawson's heyday it was said "the very air glittered with gold." There are many who would profit from the careless manner in which the treasure was spent...

No sooner was the gold out of the ground...

Than it was flung into the bars & dancehalls of Dawson.

THIS ROUND'S ON ME!

I'LL DRINK TO THAT

Some bartenders grew their fingernails to trap bits of gold.

STEP RIGHT UP FOLKS

Gold scales often rested on thick velvet (which was panned nightly).

OOPS! SORRY 'BOUT THAT...

DUMP

Some waitrons kept their hands & hair wet to secret away the treasure.

HEY, WHY IS YOUR HAIR GLOWING?

IT'S... UM... JUST THE LIGHTS IN HERE

Spilled gold created a side industry in Dawson, panning the sawdust off the saloon floors.

Many years later when old buildings were torn down, the foundations revealed a glittering surprise.

JOE! GET IN HERE QUICK.. & BRING A GOLDPAN!

GOLD DUST & GAMBLIN' FEVER

At the height of the rush, a host of gambling halls opened shop. For 24 hours (except Sundays) they were packed with eager cardhands willing to bet thousands on the drop of a card...

Here fortunes were literally lost...

STRAIGHT TAKES YOUR SET SO I NET YOUR BET.

And won overnight.

ACE TAKES YOUR STRAIGHT PAY UP, DON'T BE LATE

People began to bet on anything conceivable...

WHATS GOIN' ON?

TWPPHT

SPITTIN' CONTEST!

Here's a story of gambling gone too far. Meet Harry:

HEY HARRY, HOW MUCH DIDYA WIN?

60,000! I'M GOIN' HOME TO MONTANA, NO MORE GAMBLING FOR THIS GUY.

But his boat was delayed

SIGH!

SO... OK, I'M BACK! BUT JUST A QUICK GAME

SORRY, YOU LOSE, HARRY

WHAT ABOUT THE BOAT?

DOESN'T MATTER. HIT ME

SORRY, YOU LOSE

24 HOURS LATER... BUT HARRY, YOU'VE LOST ALL YOUR MONEY AND YOUR BOAT TICKET

MY LUCK'S GONNA CHANGE JUST PLEASE BUY MY HAT!

DANCE HALL DAYS

DOZENS OF DETERMINED DANCE HALL GIRLS HAD COMPLETED THE DIFFICULT TREK UP NORTH. AWARE THAT IT WAS EASIER TO GET GOLD FROM A MINER'S POCKET THAN THE MINE ITSELF, THEY PROSPERED AS PROSPECTORS DANCED THEIR FORTUNES AWAY...

THE STAGE WOULD BE COVERED WITH GOLD THROWN BY ENAMOURED MINERS...

AND AT 1:00 A M SHARP THE DANCING WOULD BEGIN, AT A DOLLAR A DANCE

THE DANCE HALL GIRLS WERE OFTEN ADORNED WITH SILLY NICKNAMES LIKE:

KLONDIKE KATE

SNAKE-HIPS LULU

AND DIAMOND-TOOTH GERTIE

BUT DESPITE HER SIMPLE NAME CAD WILSON WAS TO BECOME DAWSON'S FAVOURITE PERFORMER

SHE HAD THE HEAVIEST GOLD BELT IN TOWN, THANKS TO HER LEAGUE OF ADMIRERS   MORE NUGGETS? WELL... IF YOU INSIST

HER FANS ALSO REPORTEDLY FILLED A BATHTUB WITH CHAMPAGNE FOR THE "QUEEN OF THE DANCE HALLS" TO BATHE IN...

BATHING IN BUBBLY, WHO WOULDA THOUGHT..

GUARDIANS OF THE NORTH

AMIDST ALL THIS REVELRY MOVED THE MOUNTIES, WHO SINGLE-HANDEDLY SAVED DAWSON FROM BECOMING A LAWLESS & DANGEROUS TOWN LIKE SKAGWAY. SAM STEELE HAD LEFT THE MOUNTAIN PASSES & NOW RULED DAWSON WITH AN IRON FIST...

WE CORRECTLY ASSUMED GAMBLING & PROSTITUTION WOULD CONTINUE REGARDLESS OF ANY LAWS...

BUT HANDGUNS WERE STRICTLY PROHIBITED, & NOT **A SINGLE MURDER** OCCURRED IN 1898

MAJOR OFFENDERS WERE HANDED A BLUE TICKET WHICH MEANT IMMEDIATE EXPULSION FROM TOWN.

...AND STAY OUT!

MINOR OFFENDERS WERE MADE TO WORK THE WOODPILE, A JOB BOTH EXHAUSTING & EMBARRASSING

HA, HA, HA HA!

FOR 3 MONTHS ONE MISCHIEVOUS WORKER CUT THE LOGS ½ AN INCH TOO LONG TO FIT IN THE MOUNTIES' WOODSTOVE

HEE, HEE HEE

MOST, HOWEVER, LEARNED QUICKLY NOT TO MESS WITH THE MOUNTIES...

YOUR FINE IS 50 DOLLARS...

50 DOLLARS? WHY I'VE GOT THAT IN MY VEST POCKET!

...AND 60 DAYS ON THE WOODPILE DO YOU HAVE THAT IN YOUR VEST POCKET?

PRESERVE THE SABBATH

ONE LAW THAT THE MOUNTIES STRICTLY ENFORCED WAS THAT **NO ONE** WOULD WORK ON SUNDAYS. MEN WERE ARRESTED & FINED FOR INNOCENT ENOUGH TASKS LIKE FISHING & CHOPPING WOOD, SO FEW DARED LIFT A FINGER ON THE LORD'S DAY...

AT PRECISELY 12:00 MIDNIGHT ON SATURDAYS THE GAMBLING & DANCE HALLS WOULD SHUT DOWN

THIS LED ENTERPRISING DAWSONITES TO INITIATE "THE SUNDAY EXCURSION."

HEY LET'S FLOAT DOWNRIVER 50 MILES...

...INTO AMERICAN TERRITORY!

A GOLDEN OPPURTUNITY

THESE SUNDAY JOYRIDES PROVED TO BE A GREAT SUCCESS...

UNTIL ONE FATEFUL WEEKEND...

YOU MEAN TO SAY **NOBODY** BROUGHT ANY EXTRA FUEL?

UH,OH

WHAT'S UP?

CACK WHEEZE

ENGINE TROUBLE

DAWSON COULD NOW **RETURN** TO NORMAL... RELATIVELY SPEAKING, OF COURSE

BACK TO (HIC) BUSINESS

3 DAYS WENT BY & WITH OVER 400 LOCAL YOKELS GONE, THE TOWN REMAINED CLOSED... UNTIL FINALLY THE SHIPS LIMPED BACK INTO VIEW

LOOK! THERE THEY ARE!

HIGH SOCIETY

THOSE WHO HAD MADE THEIR FORTUNES FROM THE GOLD RUSH WERE MORE THAN HAPPY TO FLAUNT THAT FACT. POINTED OUT IN THE STREETS, THESE OWNERS OF SUCCESSFUL DANCE HALLS & PRODUCTIVE MINES WERE KNOWN AS "KLONDIKE KINGS."

KLONDIKE KINGS OCCUPIED THE FINEST SEATS IN THE DANCE HALLS & DRANK CHAMPAGNE AT 60 DOLLARS A QUART

SWIFTWATER BILL, MADE FAMOUS FROM THE EGG INCIDENT, ENJOYED THE LUXURY OF A PLAY BASED ON HIS EXPLOITS

...THE MONTE CARLO PROUDLY PRESENTS "THE ADVENTURES OF STILLWATER WILLIE!"

CHARLEY ANDERSON "THE LUCKY SWEDE" CASUALLY JOKED ABOUT HIS FORTUNE...

EVERYONE ALWAYS SAYS I WAS A MILLIONAIRE

...BUT THE MOST I EVER HAD WAS 900,000 DOLLARS

WHILE THE GENEROSITY OF KLONDIKE KING CLARENCE BERRY KNEW FEW LIMITATIONS

HELP YOURSELF

TAKE SOME IF YOU NEED SOME

THEN THERE WAS BIG ALEX MACDONALD, RICHEST MAN IN THE KLONDIKE, OWNER OF DOZENS OF CLAIMS, WHO WAS CONSTANTLY PURSUED BY THRONGS OF SALESMEN

CLAIM #12 ON HUNKER CREEK?

FIVE BELOW ON ELDORADO?

SWAMPLAND ON SULPHUR CREEK?

WHERE DO I SIGN?

DANCE-HALL OWNER JIM DAUGHERTY, HOWEVER, DESERVES SPECIAL ATTENTION...

THE MINI·STAMPEDE

JIM DAUGHERTY WAS A GENEROUS & TALENTED SALOON OWNER WHO LED A PACK OF PROSPECTORS ON A WILD & FROZEN GOOSE CHASE. WHY HE DID IT REMAINS UNKNOWN...

A RUMOUR HAD STARTED IN TOWN ABOUT A GOLD FIND 2 DAYS NORTH.

HEY, HAVE YOU HEARD ANYTHING ABOUT THE RICH GROUND?

YUP & JIM THERE IS THE ONLY ONE WHO KNOWS WHERE IT IS

CROWDS STARTED FOLLOWING JIM AROUND UNTIL ON JANUARY 10, 1899:

LET'S BE OFF!

SO OFF THEY WENT INTO THE NIGHT, OVER 100 EAGER PROSPECTORS FOLLOWING JIM TO HIS PROMISED LAND...

REGARDLESS OF -60°F WEATHER

ARROO!

THE FOLLOWING DAY THE GROUND WAS STAKED...

BUT NO ONE **EVER** FOUND GOLD THERE SO NEW RUMOURS BEGAN. SOME CLAIMED JIM STARTED THE MINI-RUSH ON A BET THAT NO ONE IN DAWSON COULD KEEP A SECRET. STILL OTHERS THOUGHT THAT:

JIM DAUGHERTY JUST WANTED TO KNOW IF A CHEE-CHAKO COULD OUTRUN A SOURDOUGH

WELL, DID YOU?

I'M NOT TELLING

SOURDOUGHS GO SOUTH

MANY OF THE MINERS WHO HAD STRUCK IT RICH NOW POURED OUT OF THE CREEKS & INTO THE BIG CITIES. THE PRESS WAS SOON FLOODED WITH STORIES OF THE SOURDOUGHS' WEALTH & FREE-SPENDING WAYS...

SWIFTWATER BILL ALWAYS LIKED TO MAKE A SPLASH...

OK, SO WHEN I WALK INSIDE...

LOOK! IT'S THE KING OF THE KLONDIKE!

OH, WHAT A SURPRISE!

TO THE GREAT DELIGHT OF THE PRESS, HE ONCE FILLED A BATHTUB WITH CHAMPAGNE & JUMPED IN, EXCLAIMING:

...ONE RARELY BATHES UP NORTH...

BIG ALEX WENT TO ROME & WAS KNIGHTED FOR HIS GOLDEN CONTRIBUTIONS TO THE CHURCH

BELINDA MULRONEY MARRIED A COUNT & TRAVELLED EUROPE IN STYLE

LE TAPIS ROUGE

MAGNIFIQUE

GEORGE CARMACK & HIS WIFE KATE FLAUNTED THEIR WEALTH...

GEORGE CARMACK - DISCOVERER OF KLONDIKE GOLD

CAUSING A COMMOTION WHEREVER THEY WENT.

HA, HA, HA

FREE GOLD!

MEANWHILE IN DAWSON, YET ANOTHER DISASTER WAS ABOUT TO OCCUR...

SAY... DO YOU SMELL SOMETHING BURNING?

UP IN FLAMES

DAWSON HAD BARELY SURVIVED TWO ENORMOUS FIRES IN ITS EARLY DAYS (BOTH BLAZES STARTED BY THE SAME DANCE HALL GIRL!). THIS PROMPTED LOCAL TOWNSFOLK TO RECRUIT A MUCH-NEEDED FIRE DEPARTMENT

100 MEN WERE HIRED & THE NECESSARY FIREFIGHTING EQUIPMENT PURCHASED

THEY WERE OUT OF DALMATIONS

THEN, IN APRIL 1899, THE FIREFIGHTERS WENT ON STRIKE FOR HIGHER WAGES

ONE WEEK LATER A FLAME WAS SEEN SHOOTING SKYWARD FROM A LOCAL SALOON.

FIRE!

SOON MUCH OF THE TOWN WAS GOING UP IN FLAMES

WHILE THE TEMPERATURE FELL TO -45°F, THOUSANDS DESPERATELY ATTEMPTED TO QUELL THE FLAMES

CRASH ROAR WHOOSH SMASH

COPIOUS QUANTITIES OF CASH WERE DISAPPEARING IN THE FIRE, BUT MONEY WASN'T ON EVERBODY'S MIND

GET YOUR GOLD!

TO HELL WITH THE GOLD...

SOME THINGS ARE MORE IMPORTANT!

THE NEXT DAY, WITH SOME 117 BUILDINGS DESTROYED, SOME BEGAN TO REBUILD WHILE OTHERS TRIED TO RECOUP THEIR LOSSES.

(SIGH) NEVER THOUGHT I'D BE PANNING MY OWN HOUSE

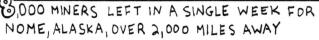

GOLD FEVER STRIKES AGAIN

THE FIRE, HOWEVER, WOULD NOT BE THE END OF DAWSON, AS NEW BUILDINGS WERE QUICKLY ERECTED. INSTEAD, THE CITY OF GOLD WOULD SUCCUMB TO THE SAME FATE THAT EMPTIED OTHER BOOM TOWNS THE NEWS OF A NEW GOLD DISCOVERY...

8,000 MINERS LEFT IN A SINGLE WEEK FOR NOME, ALASKA, OVER 2,000 MILES AWAY

GOLD! I LOVE GOLD!

BRING IT ON!

AFTER 2 YEARS IN TRANSIT, THE LAST OF THE STAMPEDERS STRAGGLED IN...

GREAT! WE FINALLY GET HERE & EVERYONE LEAVES

AT LEAST PLACES ARE CHEAP..

LATE IN 1899, A RAILROAD WAS BUILT OVER THE WHITE PASS, RENDERING THE CHILKOOT OBSOLETE

BUT IT WAS TOO LATE. MUCH OF DAWSON HAD LEFT & THE OUTSIDE HAD HAD ENOUGH OF THE GOLD RUSH

GET YOUR GOLDPANS... I MEAN DISHPANS HERE

AH, GO TO THE KLONDIKE

½ PRICE SALE

THOSE REMAINING IN DAWSON BEGAN TO MARRY & RAISE THE FIRST KLONDIKE KIDS. ONE OF THESE KIDS, PIERRE BERTON, WOULD GO ON TO BECOME ONE OF CANADA'S MOST PROMINENT AUTHORS

AND ACROSS FROM THE BERTON HOME STANDS THE LOG CABIN OF ROBERT SERVICE, WHO IMMORTALIZED THE YUKON WITH HIS PLAYFUL VERSE.

WHAT EVER HAPPENED TO....

THE GOLD FOUND IN THE KLONDIKE WAS DISPROPORTIONATE TO THE SHEER NUMBERS WHO MANAGED TO GET THERE. OF THOSE WHO DID STRIKE IT RICH ONLY THE SMALLEST HANDFUL MANAGED TO HOLD ONTO THEIR FORTUNES...

KLONDIKE KINGS BIG ALEX & JIM DAUGHERTY BOTH WENT BROKE & DIED SHORTLY AFTER THE RUSH ABATED.

THE LUCKY SWEDE'S LUCK RAN OUT. HE HAD INVESTED IN PROPERTY, ONLY TO LOSE IT IN THE 1906 SAN FRANCISCO EARTHQUAKE

BOOM! CRASH
RUMBLE   RUMBLE

ARIZONA CHARLIE CONTINUED HIS LIFE OF FOLLOWING THE ACTION...

WELCOME TO NOME ALASKA

AS DID A PENNILESS SWIFTWATER BILL, WHO WAS LAST SEEN IN PERU, WORKING IN A SILVER MINE

ALL THAT GLITTERS IS NOT GOLD

EVEN BELINDA WENT BROKE. REGARDLESS, SHE REACHED THE GRAND AGE OF 93

..IT WAS A 10 MILE WALK TO DAWSON THROUGH 7 FEET OF SNOW...

SOME, HOWEVER, REALIZED FAME & FORTUNE AFTER THE GOLDRUSH. PEOPLE LIKE PHOTOGRAPHER ERIC HEGG...

& KLONDIKE KATE. FOR YEARS HER LIVELY TALES OF DAWSON'S BAWDY DAYS ENTERTAINED THE PRESS

JACK LONDON HAD NOT STRUCK IT RICH UP NORTH, BUT MADE MILLIONS FROM HIS WEALTH OF MEMORIES

CLICK CLACK CLACK

MONEY ELUDED MOST OF THE STAMPEDERS. HOWEVER, MANY WOULD RECALL THE EXPERIENCE AS THE ADVENTURE OF THEIR LIVES

...AND I'D DO IT ALL OVER AGAIN...

THE NORTH TODAY

THE STAMPEDERS' UNIQUE LEGACY IS SEEN EVERYWHERE UP NORTH TODAY. IT IS FOUND IN THE LIVELY STORIES, THE GHOST TOWNS, THE CELEBRATIONS LIKE DISCOVERY DAY & MOST IMPORTANTLY IN A CULTURE SHAPED IN PART BY THE WORLD'S LAST GREAT GOLDRUSH

AROOOO!

THE WHITE PASS RAILWAY ALLOWS VISITORS A LEISURELY LOOK AT THE OLD STAMPEDERS' TRAIL

WHILE THE CHILKOOT PASS APPEALS TO HIKERS AROUND THE GLOBE WISHING TO RETRACE THE "TRAIL OF '98" (1,000 POUNDS OF FOOD NOT REQUIRED)

30's ENOUGH, THANKS

SKAGWAY, ONCE KNOWN AS "THE ROUGHEST PLACE IN THE WORLD", HAS MELLOWED & NOW ENJOYS A HEALTHY TOURIST TRADE

AS FOR DAWSON, THOUGH DIMINISHED IN SIZE, IT RETAINS MUCH OF ITS FRONTIER TOWN FEEL

YUP, A GOOD DAY IN THE MINES...

HEY! LET'S GO PLAY SOME BLACKJACK

YES, WE STILL ACCEPT GOLD DUST

AND ON A GOOD DAY WALKING THROUGH THE GOLD FIELDS, IF YOU ARE PATIENT & LUCKY, A GLIMPSE AT A GHOST FROM THE COLOURFUL PAST MIGHT BE YOUR REWARD.

HAPPY PROSPECTING!

THE END

About the author

Curtis Vos was born in Kingston, Ontario in 1968 and has since travelled and worked in much of Canada. One summer he hiked the Chilkoot Pass, where he got the idea for **KLONDIKE HO!**

Curtis Vos resides in the heart of the Klondike, Dawson City, where he works as a freelance artist.

BIBLIOGRAPHY

THE LAST GREAT ADVENTURE/WILLIAM BRONSON
McGRAW/HILL BOOK CO.

GHOST TOWNS OF THE YUKON
T. PATERSON / STAGECOACH

THE KLONDIKE QUEST; A PHOTOGRAPHIC ESSAY
1897-1899/PIERRE BERTON / McCLELLEND

'STROLLER WHITE'; TALES OF A KLONDIKE
NEWSMAN / ELMER J. WHITE/ MITCHELL

CHILKOOT PASS; THE MOST FAMOUS
TRAIL IN THE NORTH/ARCHIE SATTERFIELD

THE STREETS WERE PAVED WITH GOLD
STAN COHEN / PICTORIAL HISTORIES

KLONDIKE / PIERRE
BERTON/ McCLELLAND

ONE MAN'S GOLDRUSH, A KLONDIKE ALBUM
PHOTO'S BY E.A. HEGG /M. CROMWELL

THE KLONDIKE NUGGET / BANKSON
THE CAXTON PRINTERS LTD.

'HO! FOR THE KLONDIKE/JAMES B. STANTON
HANCOCK HOUSE

Fine books from Lost Moose Publishing

Another Lost Whole Moose Catalogue, A Yukon Way of Knowledge, _by the Lost Moose Collective._
"A compendious, eclectic, oversize, liberally-illustrated, off-the-wall, broadside of comment and advice on living out one's life in the Yukon" — _Books in Canada._
More than 200 northerners contributed stories, facts, photos and tips on what life's really like in the Yukon. A great read. Everybody's essential northern book: a northern bestseller.
ISBN 0-9694612-0-8

The Original Lost Whole Moose Catalogue,
A Yukon Way of Knowledge, _by the Rock and Roll Moose Meat Collective._
The classic. First published in 1979, this legendary compilation of information and anecdotes on life in the Yukon is back in print.
ISBN 0-9694612-1-6

Edge of the River, Heart of the City,
A History of the Whitehorse Waterfront, _by the Yukon Historical & Museums Association_
A loving and authoritative look back to the days of the busy waterfront in Whitehorse, where trains from the coast met sternwheelers from the Klondike at the foot of White Horse Rapids. Researched and written by Helene Dobrowolsky and Rob Ingram.
ISBN 0-9694612-2-4

Klondike Ho! _by Curtis Vos_
A cartooned history of the Klondike Gold Rush of 1896-98. Authentic, detailed, descriptive, with a touch of humour. Captures the whole mad rush in pictures and makes it easy for anyone to understand.
ISBN 0-9694612-4-0

Skookum's North _by Doug Urquhart_
A dog's-eye view of life in the north. A ten year collection of humour, warmth and insight in one great volume. Nearly 500 of the author's humorous "PAWS" comic strips published in newspapers across northern Canada and Alaska.
ISBN 0-9694612-3-2

Write to the following address for additional copies of this book, and for an up-to-date list of other books available from:

**Lost Moose Publishing
58 Kluane Crescent
Whitehorse, Yukon, Canada Y1A 3G7
Fax 403-668-6223
Phone 403-668-5076**